W 806 W'57

☑ **W9-BYZ-186**

The Life Cycle of a
Grasshopper

by Lisa Trumbauer

Consulting Editor: Gail Saunders-Smith, Ph.D.

Consultant: David H. Branson, Research Entomologist
USDA—Agricultural Research Service
Sidney, Montana

Pebble Books

an imprint of Capstone Press
Mankato, Minnesota

Pebble Books are published by Capstone Press
151 Good Counsel Drive, P.O. Box 669, Mankato, Minnesota 56002
http://www.capstone-press.com

1 2 3 4 5 6 08 07 06 05 04 03

Library of Congress Cataloging-in-Publication Data
Trumbauer, Lisa, 1963–
    The life cycle of a grasshopper / by Lisa Trumbauer.
    p. cm.—(Life cycles)
    Includes bibliographical references and index.
    Summary: Describes the physical characteristics, habits, and stages of
development of grasshoppers.
    ISBN 0-7368-2089-2 (hardcover)
    1. Grasshoppers—Life cycles—Juvenile literature. [1. Grasshoppers.] I. Title.
II. Life cycles (Mankato, Minn.)
QL508.A2 T78 2004
595.7'26—dc21   2002154713

Note to Parents and Teachers

The Life Cycles series supports national science standards related
to life science. This book describes and illustrates the life cycle of
a short-horned grasshopper. The images support early readers in
understanding the text. The repetition of words and phrases helps
early readers learn new words. This book also introduces early
readers to subject-specific vocabulary words, which are defined in
the Words to Know section. Early readers may need assistance to
read some words and to use the Table of Contents, Words to
Know, Read More, Internet Sites, and Index/Word List sections
of the book.

(Table of Contents

Photographs in this book show the life cycle of a short-horned grasshopper.

summer

pod

4

Egg

A grasshopper begins life
as an egg in a pod.

spring

Nymph

A nymph hatches from the egg in spring. A nymph is a young grasshopper.

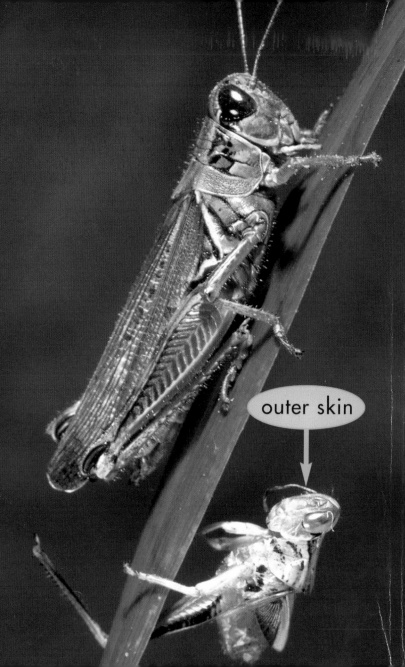

outer skin

The nymph molts many times. It sheds its outer skin to grow.

2 months

Adult

The nymph becomes
an adult. Most adult
grasshoppers live
for 50 days.

Adult grasshoppers use their long legs to jump. They have wings.

Male grasshoppers make a sound with their legs. The sound attracts a female. The two grasshoppers mate.

The female grasshopper digs a hole in the ground. She lays eggs in the hole.

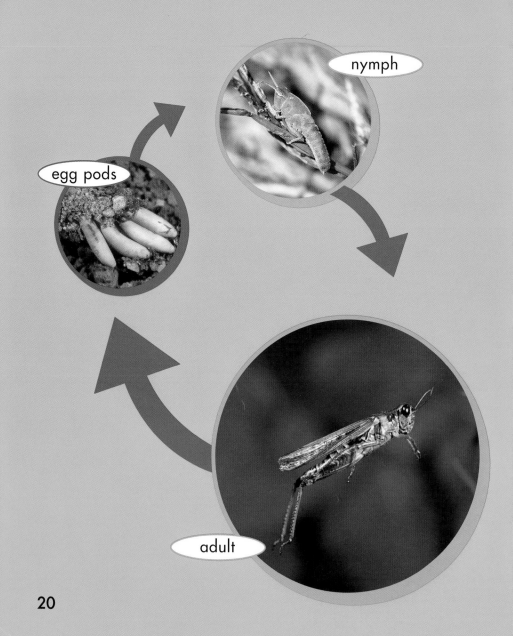

nymph

egg pods

adult

20

The Life Cycle

The eggs are the start
of a new life cycle.

Words to Know

adult—an animal that is able to mate

attract—to get the attention of someone or something

egg—a small case in which a grasshopper grows; short-horned grasshoppers lay many eggs together in a pod; there are about 18 eggs in each pod.

hatch—to break out of an egg; female grasshoppers lay eggs in summer; grasshopper nymphs hatch in spring.

life cycle—the stages of life of an animal; the life cycle includes being born, growing up, having young, and dying.

mate—to join together to produce young

molt—to shed skin so that new skin can grow; nymphs molt at least five times as they grow.

nymph—a young grasshopper that changes into an adult by shedding its skin many times

(Read More

Allen, Judy, and Tudor Humphries. *Are You a Grasshopper?* Backyard Books. New York: Kingfisher, 2002.

Hovanec, Erin M. *I Wonder What It's Like to Be a Grasshopper.* A Life Science Wonder Book. New York: PowerKids Press, 2000.

Zuchora-Walske, Christine. *Leaping Grasshoppers.* Pull Ahead Books. Minneapolis: Lerner, 2000.

(Internet Sites

Do you want to find out more about grasshoppers? Let FactHound, our fact-finding hound dog, do the research for you.

Here's how:

1) Visit *http://www.facthound.com*

2) Type in the **Book ID** number: **0736820892**

3) Click on **FETCH IT**.

FactHound will fetch Internet sites picked by our editors just for you!

Index/Word List

Word Count: 108
Early-Intervention Level: 13

Editorial Credits

Sarah L. Schuette, editor; Kia Adams, series designer; Jennifer Schonborn, interior
    designer; Enoch Peterson, production designer; Kelly Garvin, photo researcher;
    Karen Risch, product planning editor

Photo Credits

Corbis/Rob C. Nunnington; Gallo Images, 16
Courtesy of Charles S. Lewallen, cover (nymph), 6, 20 (top)
Dwight R. Kuhn, cover (adult), 1, 4, 8, 10, 12, 14, 18, 20 (left, bottom)